SHEDONISM

noun

1   The belief that all people have the right to do everything in their power to achieve the greatest amount of pleasure possible to them, in a shed.

2   A joyous utilitarianism, or an aesthetic of sensual materialism, in a space adjacent to (and separate from) main activity centres.

She had a lifelong commitment to shedonism.

SHEDONISM

101 Excuses to Escape to Your Shed

Ben Williams

with illustrations by William Finch

POP PRESS

Contents

Introduction

Approaching down the garden path, fumbling with the padlock, flicking the latch, groping around in the dark. To enter the shed is to enter another dimension. For some, this will mean a portal to a Narnia-type world, a costume change à la Mr Benn – and a transgression. For others, it will be somewhere to keep the old lawnmower.

Either way, the shed is a rare private place in a hyper-connected world, somewhere to indulge yourself with hobbies that will seem boring and outdated to some – but what matter? There is no such thing as shame in your shed.

Indeed, boredom or the associated free unravelling of your mind, disgorging yourself of the day's accounts; reclaiming time, back from the tyranny of enforced hours – this is to be encouraged in your shed. Here one might lose days whittling (p. 93). This is a place to make inconsequential decisions over an extended period, with activity measured only by the brew time of a homemade mug (p. 130) of homemade herbal tea (p. 72).

But this is not only a book about mindfulness, as those seeking to butcher a rabbit (p. 29) or prepare for a nuclear apocalypse (p. 180) will usefully discover.

The shed might traditionally signify the nostalgic and the male, somewhere to fart in peace or store outmoded items. This book signals the dawning of a new, metrosexual golden age of craft. For as well as traditional artisan practices, such as embossing leather goods (p. 98) or installing a model village (p. 138), you will find a rough guide to preserving (p. 17), curing

(p. 26), smoking (p. 21), raising (p. 34) and popping up (p. 49).

If it turns out to be a sly political tract, a kind of manifesto of wholesome activity, then this only reflects what shedders worldwide are actually doing now. Similarly if the book has an ecological bent – this reinforces the idea that the shed is noble, and that shedders are a noble breed.

There is also evidence of the consummately modern, and here you will find guidance on how to vlog (p. 197), make a dance record (p. 192), slime (p. 173), and hack (p. 205). The digital world creeps in.

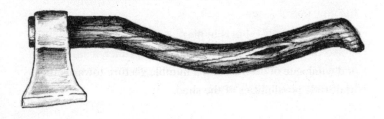

'Approaching down the garden path, fumbling with the padlock, flicking the latch, groping around in the dark. To enter the shed is to enter another dimension.'

And despite the book having discrete
sections ('Arts & Crafts' etc), you are
encouraged to free-associate the
entries – to remove the plastic
packaging, if you will – and
explore the relationship between
seemingly odd elements. Here
you will be encouraged to cure
meat (p. 26) and preserve an
animal skull (p. 165), almost in
the same breath. You might make a
squirrel trap (p. 149) but also create a bird-watching
hide (p. 152).
In the shed, everything is in play.

So this book is at once a guide and a primer, a stimulus
and catalogue of desires, and a humble gesture towards the
multitude possibilities of the shed.

FOOD
&
DRINK

1.

Preserve lemons

Preserving fruit is an essential skill for the paranoiac (*see* nuclear bunker, p. 180) but also a voguish way to mitigate the effects of any social or political upheaval.

Clean your jars assiduously with soapy water, then put them in a cooling oven to dry. Scrub a number of unwaxed lemons, cut them in half lengthways, then divide each half into three long slices. Pack these tightly into the sterilised jars and pour a load of sea salt around them. Add cinnamon sticks, a couple of red chillies and bay leaves if desired. Press it all down and finish with another layer of salt. Put them in your shed and rotate the jars daily; mature lemons will be yellowish-brown. Once opened, pour a layer of olive oil on top to keep them cured. These are very good when eaten with rice and white fish.

2.
Hang game

If veganism is the apogee of ethical eating, then hunting and preparing your own kill is surely not too far behind. To look into their misty eyes, and to pluck them, is to radically engage with your dinner in a way that a plastic-packed chicken breast could never recreate.

The shed is an ideal place to hang game birds. This is necessary to purge the animal of the adrenaline it used to take off, before it was shot, as well as rest the bird: this helps to develop flavours.

Dangle the birds from the neck to prevent fluids pooling, and improvise a sort of net curtain surround to ward off flies. How long you hang them depends on age, but between two and four days seems to be the norm. Ideally your shed should be cool – around 4°C – although anything under 15°C is fine.

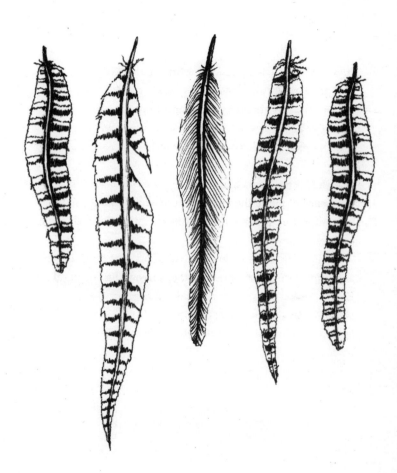

3.
Hot smoking

Hot smoking is a delicious way to sophisticate simple foods, and best done in the shed where you can safely corral the aromas.

Mackerel or trout is a good place to start. Salt the fish: this draws moisture from the flesh and makes the smoky taste more profound. Scatter a generous layer of flaky or coarse salt over a large plate, put your fish on top, then add a further layer of salt. How long you leave it depends on the fish: small specimens might need 10 minutes, a big fish more like 40. After the appropriate time, rinse the fish thoroughly and pat dry with kitchen towel.

For the smoking you can use an old metal bread bin, but a large, snugly-lidded saucepan also works. Bodge a metal smoking rack out of whatever you have around; this will need to sit neatly about 10 centimetres above the bottom of the smoker. Experiment with different wood chips for different flavours, but make sure to use non-resinous, untreated woods like alder, beech or cherry.

Open the windows and door of your shed for ventilation, then put your smoker – lid on – onto a stove at high heat. When it starts to smoulder, turn it down low and put your fish on the rack until it is cooked as you like it. You can smoke meat or poultry in the same way.

4.
Growing rhubarb

The Rhubarb Triangle is an area in West Yorkshire littered with dark sheds chock-full of tender 'forced rhubarb', which 'pops' mysteriously as it grows. This somewhat alien, rubbery plant is grown by candlelight, and we might think of the process as a cruel but romantic type of vegan theatre.

Growing rhubarb is straightforward, and the process easily replicated in your ad hoc forcing shed. But do allow the plant to develop outside for a couple of years first, so it can take in energy through photosynthesis. Then dig it up in early winter and pot it up in your warmer, lightless shed, where it will grow vociferously.

5.
Growing mushrooms

You can go deep on this otherworldly species, which (much like rhubarb, *see* p. 22) is ideally suited to the alternate universe of your shed. If you wish to create an off-grid DIY mushroom-fruiting chamber, then be prepared to employ the following:

an old glass fridge door
about 3 litres of grain spawn
3 pillowcases
rope
a clean brick.

An easier option is to take pre-pasteurised substrate and dump it out onto a nice clean surface in your shed. Then take a bag of broken-up mushroom spawn and sprinkle it the length of the substrate. Mix it up evenly with clean hands.

Pack the inoculated substrate into mushroom bags, jars or buckets. Seal and put into a warm dark corner. Look to keep your shed at a cosy 20°C.

Your creation could be ready to fruit in as little as a few weeks. When your substrate is white with mycelium, you know it's ready. Now open the container and ventilate your shed – getting some airflow through and cooling the temperature a little – and watch your fungi flourish.

6.
Cure meat

They say that the erstwhile joys of smoking tobacco were discovered by primitive man, who literally fell into a smouldering pile of the addictive leaf. The same rough serendipity is probably at the root of curing, the ancient method of preserving meat.

A dead animal was found washed ashore and hadn't rotted, and although the meat was salty, grey and disgusting, nobody died after consuming it. This was a Neolithic lightbulb (or equivalent) moment: salt, or more accurately saltpetre, preserves food. Today curing salts – specially prepared blends of salt and sodium nitrate – are widely used.

To cure your own bacon, remove all skin from 1.5 kilograms of unsliced belly pork, running a knife between the skin and the fat. Combine 4 ½ teaspoons of salt, the same of ground black pepper, 6 tablespoons of dark brown sugar, ¾ cup of distilled water and ½ teaspoon of the essential Prague Powder #1, then pour it into a large plastic zipper bag.

Seal the bag and slosh everything about until it is well mixed. Now add the belly. Remove as much air as possible and massage the cure into the meat, making sure all sides are coated. Place it in a fridge at 1–3°C, massaging the bag every day to keep the pork marinating. After three to five days, remove the pork from the bag and throw the liquid away. Rinse off any thick deposits of salt.

Now get the meat in your shed and into your smoker (the internal temperature should be about 65°C), for two hours. You can use any wood you like but hickory is king. After smoking, slice off the ends – which will be very dark and heavily seasoned – and taste right away.

7.

Butcher a rabbit

Having hung game in your shed (*see* p. 18) and forced rhubarb (*see* p. 22), this process will take you one step closer to subsistence.

Butchery is a dark art – one we usually turn from and delegate – but mastering it will surely enlighten us (*see* preserve a skull, p. 165). Rabbit is delicious, but does require a little more preparation than your average chicken. You will need a very sharp boning knife, a pair of kitchen shears and a cleaver.

Remove any silver skin and sinew – then remove the front legs, which aren't attached to anything by bone. Throughout the butchering process, continue to remove and discard anything that doesn't look good.

Hind legs are the money cut here, so slice gently along the pelvic bone until you get to the joints. Pop the joint and slice around the back leg to free it from the carcass.

Once you've done both legs, you are left with the loin. Portion it by removing the pelvis – bash it with the cleaver and contort the carcass, followed by some subtle use of the boning knife. Snip off the ribs with your shears. Now chop the loin into bite-size pieces, hit it with some Kentucky spices and fry it up for a tasty treat.

8.
Making sloe gin

**Any forager who has plucked the sloe, and sucked it –
mistaking it for a damson, their lips disappearing into their
face – will know that these astringent suckers need some
treatment. And what better treatment than gin.**

Autumn is the time for this fruit of the blackthorn, and they
are ripest for picking when there is a dusty chalk on the
purple fruit. Pick those that have ripened in the sun, as they
will be sweeter than those grown in the shade.

It's then easy to create a sultry liqueur that's equally good
for medievalists, and when drizzled across a cake. Firstly,
remove any stems before putting the sloes in a freezer
overnight. Next day, take an airtight jar that holds 1.5 litres,
add the frozen sloes and 250 grams of sugar, plus 70 centilitres
of gin. Keep the jar in a dark corner of your shed for at least
three months – or as long as you can bear – before drinking
and rotate it a few times during the early weeks.

Shedonism

9.

Brew your own beer

You may think that brewing is fiendishly complicated and that your efforts may result only in some embarrassing and potentially poisonous slop. And while weird scientists have the best brews – the internet is a Pandora's box of obscure secrets – it *is* possible for non-geeks to get the basics. These are:

1. Soak barley in hot water to release the malt sugars.
2. Boil this solution with hops for seasoning.
3. Cool and add yeast to begin fermentation.
   (This ferments the sugars, releasing CO_2 and ethyl alcohol.)
4. Bottle the beer with a bit of added sugar to provide carbonation.

It is possible to fit out your shed with all the necessary equipment – brew pots, fermenters and siphons – for less than £100, and from brewing to consuming can take as little as a month.

10.
Raise chickens

Those not yet at the smallholding stage will recognise the chicken as a symbol of both self-sufficiency and the bohemian life.

So fit out your shed with nesting boxes (where the chickens will lay their eggs) made from any uniformly sized crates. Put these into a wooden frame made from salvaged materials. Find space for your roost – basically a wide ladder laid at a shallow angle – where the birds will sleep. Add water and a feeder, and put a large cat or dog flap in one corner of your shed so the birds can get into the run. Chickens make a mess, so scatter the floor liberally with sawdust.

Chickens can also very quickly and efficiently destroy a newly planted garden, so even if you want your birds to range freely then it's still a good idea to build them a run. This gives that bit of control at dawn or dusk when the birds like to be outside, and provides protection against foxes.

11.
Birch sap syrup

Birch sap is in truth a fairly tasteless liquid, and the joy of it lies in the collection. Be inspired by a clutch of mature silver birch trees near to your home. This is a chance to commune with nature, albeit drill in hand.

Use a hand drill to make a slightly upward-slanting hole at waist height, of about 5 centimetres. If nothing emerges, you are at the wrong tree, or the right tree at the wrong time: birch sap rises during a two-week window, usually around mid-March, but this is variable depending on location and weather.

When you strike sap, hammer in a spigot, hook your bucket over the top and cover the whole with a cloth. Return the next day to collect your sap. Remember to carefully plug the hole you have made with a tailored wooden plug.

To make pancake syrup, boil the sap in a large pan over a stove until reduced by half, then transfer to a bain-marie and reduce again until you're left with 10 per cent of what you started with. Strain through a muslin cloth and add sugar to sweeten the syrup.

12.
Make an oil-drum barbeque

The rise of the maudlin gas-powered barbeque has reduced a one-time fire ceremony to huddling around a grill. Fortunately it is quick and easy to literally salvage the true spirit of the event by appropriating an oil drum from your local garage and transforming it into an ad hoc yard-style cooker.

First, give the thing a rinse-down and drain out as much oil as possible. Then draw a 135-degree segment on the circular ends, using a marker pen and a straight edge, and join them up across the drum. This section will be your foldable lid.

Drill a hole somewhere on your line. This will be the starting point for cutting, so make it large enough to get a jigsaw blade in. Now use a jigsaw with a metal-cutting blade to steadily remove the marked section. Wear ear defenders and let the saw do the work. You may need an extra pair of hands to stop the drum from shifting around.

Use kitchen towel to wipe any residual oil from the inside of the drum, and fold over any sharp edges (this is easily done with pliers). Drill holes in the base of the drum for ventilation.

Light a fire in the drum to burn off any last bits of oil, then put some old bricks in the base. For an authentic finish, prop your barrel on a pile of yet more bricks.

13.

Making elderflower cordial

The elder was long regarded as a sacred tree, protected by the Elder Mother who lived in its trunk, and many country folk would refuse to cut or burn the wood for fear of upsetting her. Picking the sweetly scented, creamy white flowers – and turning them into a terrific aromatic cordial – might rather be thought of as a homage. This recipe makes about 2 litres.

Gather 25 elderflower heads on a warm, dry day. At home, remove any insects, then place the heads in a large bowl, adding the zest of one orange and three lemons. Boil 1.5 litres of water on the stove and pour it into the bowl. Cover and leave overnight to infuse.

Strain the liquid through a piece of muslin into a saucepan. Add 1 kilogram of sugar, plus the juice of the lemons and orange. Heat gently to dissolve the sugar, bring to a simmer and cook for a couple of minutes.

Use a funnel to pour the hot syrup into sterilised bottles. Seal the bottles with swing-top lids, sterilised screw-tops or corks. Once the potion is cool, it is ready to drink.

14.
Grow salad in a pallet

If your garden is ornamental or taken up mostly by your shed, then growing edibles may seem off limits. But there is another way to grow tasty plants – vertically. Spinach, rocket and red leaf lettuce all take kindly to being grown in this way.

Take an old pallet – heat-treated, and definitely not chemically treated – and cover the bottom, back and sides with landscape fabric; this stops the soil and plants from falling out. Use a staple gun to fix this around the edges, making sure the fabric is very taut.

Lay the pallet flat so that you can fill it. Put the plants in the arrangement you want, packing them tightly so they'll stay in place. Fill the surrounding areas with compost.

Leave the pallet flat for a few weeks, watering it regularly so the roots can grow and bed in. This means the plants will stay in place when you come to hoist the pallet up in a sunny corner of the garden.

15.
Making kimchi

They say that Koreans eat it literally every day, with every meal: 'kimchi' is basically a catch-all term for fermented vegetables of any type, but the traditional napa cabbage kimchi is the one most Westerners know. The shed is a great place for pungent experimentations. You will need a big jar.

First, prepare your cabbage; this is a loving process and requires patience. Score it lengthwise into quarters, and then slowly separate it by hand. Thoroughly bathe each cabbage quarter in salt water, one at a time, then shake off the excess liquid. Sprinkle salt generously over the thick white part of each leaf.

Prepare the seasoning ingredients, which will also aid fermentation. *Saeu-jeot* (salted shrimp) and *myeolchi-jeot* (salted anchovies) are the two that are most commonly used, in addition to ginger and Korean chilli-pepper flakes. Mix with julienned radish, pear and shallots.

Place one cabbage quarter in the jar with the seasoning mix. Spread the mix over each leaf, using one to two tablespoons for large leaves. Repeat with the remaining cabbage pieces. Once all the cabbage pieces are in the jar, press down hard to remove any air pockets. Rinse the bowl that contained the spice mix with half a cup of water and pour this liquid over the kimchi.

Leave out at room temperature for a full day or two, depending on how fast you want your kimchi to ripen, then store in the fridge. Kimchi needs about two weeks in the fridge to fully develop its flavours.

16.
Making kombucha

Kombucha is a mysterious drink, on first acquaintance a sort of carbonated vinegary tea – but not unpleasant for that. You may have tried it at a boutique festival. Kombucha contains the probiotic elements essential for those paying careful attention to their digestion.

Making it is easy but you will first need to get your hands on the mythical SCOBY ('Symbiotic Cultures of Bacteria and Yeast'), the lumpen mass of bacteria and yeast that puts fizz into your drink. You can buy one of these creatures online or secure a slice from a friendly local Kombucha purveyor. Also get some starter liquid, packed with bacteria, which will kickstart your brew. The rest is easy. This makes a one-gallon batch.

Make a pot of tea using 4 cups of water and 2 tablespoons of loose black tea. Steep for 5–10 minutes. Strain the tea into a gallon container and stir in one cup of pure cane sugar. Now top up the container with water until nine tenths full. Let this all cool to room temperature. Now place your SCOBY on top and pour in the starter liquid. Cover with a clean tea towel and clamp this on with a rubber band.

The temperature at which you store your concoction is key to the success or otherwise of your brew: between 24–29°C (75–85F) is ideal. On top of your fridge or freezer may be perfect. Your Kombucha will take between one and three weeks to ferment. The SCOBY may disfigure spectacularly during this time, with replicants and fronds forming. Nevertheless, poke a paper straw past this, in deep, and keep tasting until you are happy.

Remove the SCOBY and keep a cup or two of starter liquid for your next batch. Now bottle (washer-topped, reusable wine bottles are good), seal and leave at room temperature for two to four days before chilling and drinking.

17.
Turn your shed into a wine cellar

You are buying too much wine, it's getting seriously out of hand. You have a problem. Where do you keep all the wine?

Before storing wine in your shed, install a high-quality insulation product and vapour barrier on walls, ceiling and floor. This will help prevent moisture from entering, and potentially damaging your collection. Be aware that sunlight can damage wine.

The basic rule of wine storage is that the cooler wine is kept, the slower – and possibly the more interestingly – it will develop. But what you need in your DIY cellar-shed is *consistency* of temperature. The ideal is 10–15°C.

18.

Pop-up restaurant

Putting a restaurant in your shed is in line with the experiential trend – consider keeping stray rakes – but also fits neatly within a retail environment that favours the nimble pop-up. You will follow in the footsteps of Solo per Due, in the countryside north of Rome, which has only two seats. And the windowless London eatery where eight sit opposite the chef. Your shed restaurant will be all about intimacy and 'breaking down boundaries' – but watch out when frying hot courgette flowers.

Embrace garden produce and don't be afraid to serve a lettuce course. Modern restaurant promotion is all about seeding a reputation on sites such as TripAdvisor, so begin by penning a load of fake reviews. Hotspots are all about quirks, so cut through the noise and come up with a killer concept, like serving dishes on recycled garden implements.

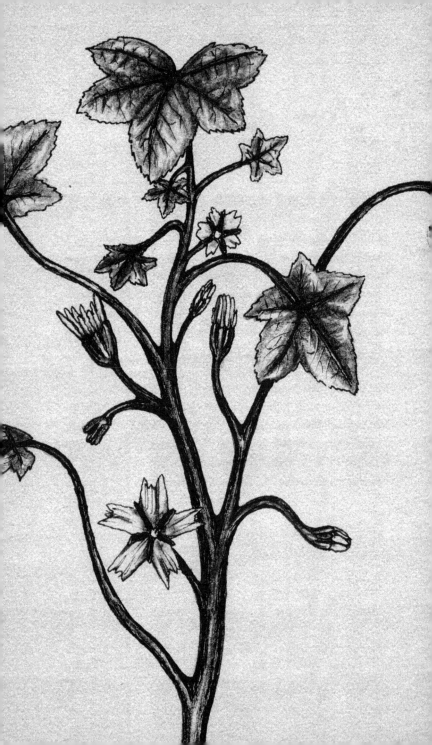

HEALTH
&
WELLBEING

19.
Far niente

This book is full of distractions and follies, a shoring-up of fragments against the tide of the modern world. It is a catalogue of indifference to obliged responsibility.

But what if there is a purer kind of solace or absence that one might seek in a shed? This entry is the rough equivalent of lying face down on a beach.

In all of us there is a desire to do literally nothing – the opposite to mindfulness. The Italians have a phrase for it: *far niente* ('doing nothing') or more fully *dolce far niente* (roughly, 'sweet idleness'). Compare the French noun *fainéant*, more like 'lazybones', a short step away from the almost-complimentary *flâneur* – a term for the literary loafer.

Before we get carried away, a definition from comedian Micky Flanagan involves swishing water around mindlessly in a bath.

Running a bath isn't possible in a shed, but try:

- Raking your hand across a small cardboard box full of old nails

- Picking through an assorted carton of nuts and bolts – do not be tempted to sort

- Flicking through a box of 1970s furniture magazines in a foreign language

- Kicking a tyre.

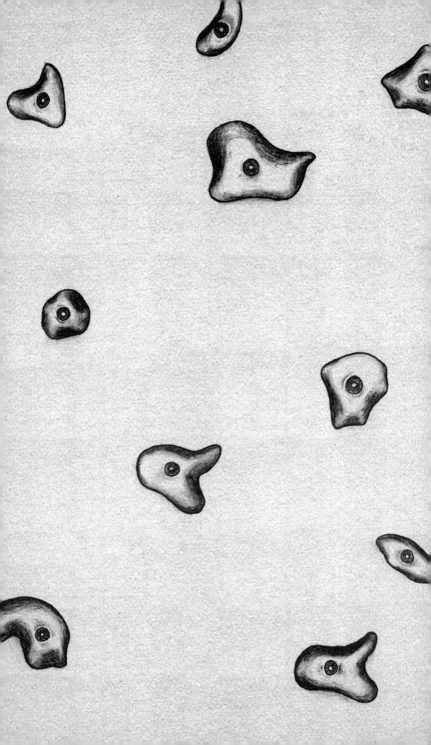

20.
Climbing gym

Despite its origins in mountaineering, rock climbing may now be the ultimate city sport. This is in part down to the rise of the climbing gym, where body-conscious urbanites can watch one another spidering around in tight trousers. Rock climbing is also a way of keeping fit without conspicuously trying to keep fit.

Yet to get to the next level you will need to embark on simple, boring routines. And what better space for this than the shed. Strong fingers are key to hard climbing, so put up a fingerboard – a sculpted wooden or plastic frame with edges and pockets of various sizes – and find a routine online. You will basically be dangling by your fingers; don't overdo it.

Aim for a well-rounded fitness programme. Thin climbing savant Adam Ondra is a flexible wizard, so get a yoga mat and try the Eagle Pose, or the Tree Pose. You should also work on general conditioning, so lots of different exercises with low-weight dumbbells, and fairly high reps.

21.
Shed sauna

We admire many aspects of Scandinavian culture, from gritty crime thrillers to pickled herring. Yet the sauna is still somehow the preserve of health spas, or the scene of seedy Soho solicitations. In an overcrowded world, they also occupy a kind of gratuitous space. Enter the shed.

First insulate your shed using wood fibre or rolled fibreglass on the walls, ceiling and door. You'll need a moisture barrier too; heavy-duty aluminium foil is effective. Coat your entire space with the shiny side facing the interior.

It is possible to buy tongue-and-groove wall boards made especially for saunas, but those on a budget should shop around lumber yards for any appropriate stuff, then shiplap your own. Traditionally, everything is made of spruce or pine. This needs to be bone-dry so that it will not shrink when the sauna is in use.

Buying a specific sauna heater makes the heating quite straightforward; just install according to the manufacturer's instructions. Some sauna owners obsess over venting, but others just use a wide gap under the door with a vent at the other end of the shed.

It is quite feasible to do nothing to your floor and for your sauna still to work. Otherwise there are a multitude of options, from laying concrete boards to installing ceramic tiles or vinyl. Either way, lay a removable duckboard on top – this is the traditional slatted sauna floor – in whichever wood you wish.

22.
A modern shrine

One might argue that online technologies are but a shrine to ourselves (*see* vlogging, p. 197). Brits are historically suspicious of shrines and icons. Yet, in a sign of changing times, there is a newfangled British Pilgrimage Trust, set up to encourage wandering between our traditional holy places.

If converting your shed, sashay past the clichés and avoid pseudo-mystical clutter such as candles and incense. Shrines have often been found at the headwaters of rivers, so get a mini water feature which can tinkle away gently in a corner of your shed. Erect an altar. The shrine is fundamentally a place where we prepare ourselves for transport to another world, so be sure to include clay birds, horses and ships, the TV remote, fish fingers and a copy of the *Daily Mail*.

23.
Essential oils

Essential oils are a key part of the homeopath's tool kit, rescued from the hippy. You can probably find them at your local farmers' market, but they're often expensive. Why not make your own? You don't need a huge amount of equipment to exploit the healing power of your garden.

You can use all sorts of plants, from herbs and scented flowers to fruits. Peppermint, rose and lavender are all things you might reasonably be able to source.

'Essential' really means 'essence' and you'll need a lot of your chosen raw material to produce a decent concentration. To extract the essence, pack a jar full of lavender, then fill it with vodka until the petals are submerged. Place this in a dark corner of your shed where it can sit undisturbed. Give the jar a good shake a couple of times a day until you see the petals begin to lose their colour.

When this happens, pass the mixture through a porcelain-coated strainer; be careful not to spill any liquid. Now tip the lavender onto a cheesecloth, squeezing it by hand to get every last bit of vodka out. Soak a new batch of lavender in the same (increasingly foul-smelling) vodka. The more often you can repeat this, the more essence your liquid will contain.

Finally put the pure, plant-free solution back into the jar and leave it undisturbed for a day or two. You will notice the vodka beginning to separate from the essential oils and any remaining plant matter. Now freeze the jar – vodka does not freeze, so only the essential oils and plant stuffs will solidify.

On bottling day, move fast before it all melts. Skim off the essential gunk and place it on top of a piece of muslin inside a glass bowl. Pour what's left of the liquid into another glass jar with a loose muslin stretched across it; any frozen, non-plant matter is the good stuff. Carefully add all essential gunk into a classic dropper bottle.

24.
Get hench

The shed is an ideal venue for a fitness studio, a space to steal a moment away from your busy schedule. This is better for those people who train best alone; some of us are inspired by watching other people sweat.

Make sure you install a foam floor, or use multiple yoga mats, and bring the old stereo out from the house. Otherwise a mindful approach to equipping your shed will pay dividends, so don't bother with faddy stuff off QVC. Instead, prioritise a basic barbell and plate set. These will allow you to train:

Legs: Front squat, back squat, lunges, deadlift

Back: Barbell row, upright row, power clean

Shoulders: Military press, behind-the-neck press

Chest: Bench press (flat, incline and decline)

Arms: Bicep curls, skull crushers, close-grip bench press

Pin up a few posters of Arnold Schwarzenegger in his *Pumping Iron* prime, and aim also to look like a sculpture made from lightly toasted chicken fillets.

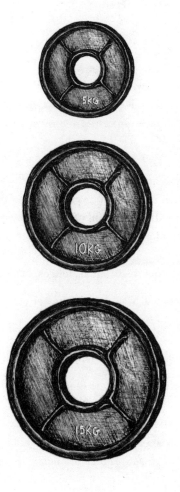

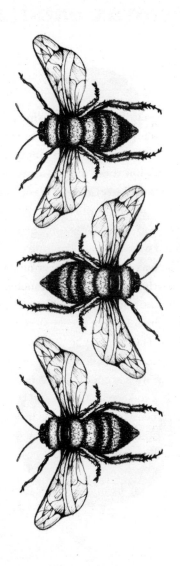

25.

Beeswax candles

What better way to set off your shed shrine (*see* p. 59) than with a beeswax candle, especially if you've taken the wax from your own bees (*see* p. 162). You may have similar candles in the home, but these often contain paraffin and other nasties, so it's well worth making your own.

Place sufficient beeswax into a large can, then put this inside a stockpot half-filled with water. Add a little coconut oil to the can, to thin out the wax, and simmer over medium–high heat on a gas burner, stirring occasionally as it melts.

Meanwhile, prepare your jars and wicks. The aim is to get the wick to stay in the middle of the jar as you pour in the beeswax and it sets. The best way to do this is to place a dab of glue on the bottom of the wick to secure it to the bottom of the jar, then curl the wick around a pencil laid across the top of the jar to keep it... to keep it straight and standing up.

Pour the melted beeswax into the jars, leaving an inch of space at the top. Set the jars aside and allow them to cool and set completely. Finally, trim the wick.

26.
Apple face mask

The humble apple has slipped behind the goji berry in the English imagination, and it's not uncommon to see them rotting on the trees come autumn. So why not ask the landowners – or do some old-fashioned scrumping – and turn your forage into a refreshing face mask.

Apples are good for cosmetics as they contain alpha hydroxy acids (AHAs), which help break down the gum that holds onto dead skin cells. Dissolving this gum releases the cells so they can be washed away.

To create your mask, peel, core and grate one apple. Add 2 teaspoons of hazelnut oil and 1 teaspoon of glycerine, then mix until smooth. Put this on your face for 15 minutes, then rinse with warm water. Follow up with plenty of mallow moisturiser (*see* p. 80), which will be readily absorbed by the fresh skin you've uncovered.

27.

Gong bath

The gong is an instrument whose sound you can immerse yourself in, providing a shortcut to a calm mind for those who find it hard to meditate. This is a team effort, so recruit a fellow aspiring Buddhist to help.

Firstly, strip back your shed to the bare essentials, as for *far niente* (*see* p. 52). Make sure that you can achieve a comfortable horizontal position, and fit out your shed with a yoga mat and pillow, as well as a blanket.

Appropriate noise is created through a mixture of gongs (in your shed, a smaller gong is advisable), chimes and singing bowls, to create an obscure symphony that will carry you away.

'If there is demand in your area, then what better use for your shed than to fit it out as a nail salon?'

28.
Nail salon

A walk through much of subtopian Britain will reveal a cheap mosaic of nail bars, discount meat warehouses and charity shops. As such, the nail bar will – for some – be a sign of urban malaise.

Yet if there is demand in your area, then what better use for your shed than to fit it out as a nail salon?

Keep an eye on local competitors to establish their strengths and weaknesses, and to find your niche. Are nearby salons catering to the cheaper end of the market? If so, there may be space for a conspicuously luxurious nail shed.

You will need a manicure table as well as a selection of nail polish and tools; consider installing motorised vents to pull away fumes. It's important to properly dry clients' nails after polishing to prevent smudging, so consider investing in a drying lamp.

29.
Herbal tea
emporium

Allium flowers, bee balm, hibiscus blossoms, hollyhock, Johnny-jump-ups, chickweed, dandelions and goldenrod. Good King Henry. Herbal teas made from these help to strengthen the immune system and detoxify the body; they are loaded with vitamins, antioxidants and essential oils. Your garden – or even the waste ground near your house – probably has a lot of stuff in it that you can turn into tea.

Your shed is the perfect repository for your collection of picked and dried plants. This is an ideal project when combined with the home library (*see* p. 179).

A few dandelion greens and flowers – or raspberry leaves for a sweeter taste – serve as a great base; add the same quantity of whatever you can forage from the list above. Experiment, as the quantity you use will depend on taste. Put these into a big pot or a sparkling-clean cafetière, pour boiling water on top and leave to steep for a few minutes, before straining.

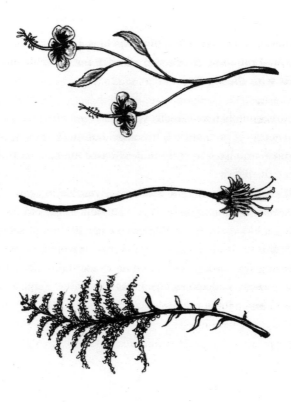

30.
Restore a vintage bicycle

Stripped to its basic idea, the bicycle is a triumph of form and function. It is a sign of what can be achieved solely with the legs.

Restoring an old bike is really about process. You may think this smacks of premature retirement, but this is great therapy for those who have to perform desk-based mental acrobatics during the day.

It's reassuring just how much you'll be able to figure out simply by contemplating (or dismantling) the machine. Buying a bicycle in the worst possible condition may seem counter-intuitive but it is really the best way of discovering its intricacies. Also, older bikes don't require the specialist tools of today, and you can go a long way with an adjustable spanner and a lot of rubbing.

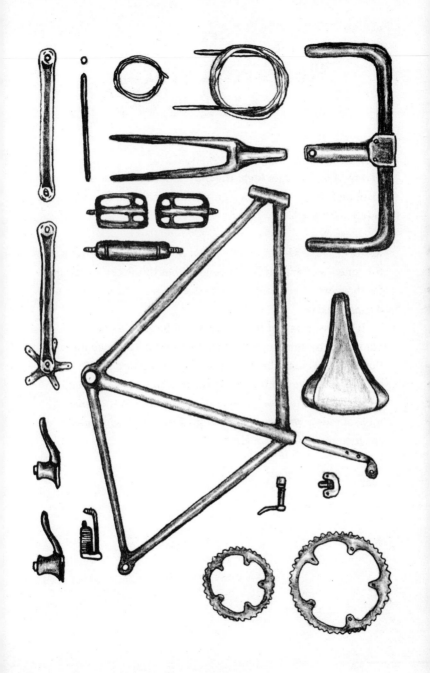

31.
Log sunlounger

If the plastic sunlounger brings to mind package holidays, sticky backs and presumptuous foreigners, then why not reclaim the design and make your own out of logs?

You can make this piece cheaply out of waste wood reclaimed from landscaping projects. Firstly, cut your logs into 18-inch sections. (For the sake of practicality, your logs should be between 3 and 6 inches in diameter.) Then draw the full-size outline of your lounger on a large piece of paper on the floor. Go for a sinuous, modern shape rather than copying the rickety plastic model currently folded up in the corner of your shed. The outline will allow you to see the logs in the correct arrangement before you start drilling and screwing.

Now it is all about fixing the logs together. Using a 1-¼" bit, drill 1–2 inches into one log. Then use zinc-coated lag screws (6–9 inches long, depending on the girth of the log) and drill through and into the second log to attach them. Attempt to get the lag screw at least 2.5 inches into the second log. Each pair of logs should be connected by 3–4 screws.

Once you've finished attaching all the logs, flip the chair over and see if it wobbles in a specific place. You can use steel brackets and deck screws on the bottom of the lounger to strengthen and stiffen the weak and wobbly parts.

32.
Marshmallow
hand cream

The word 'marshmallow' derives from the Old English
***malwe* (meaning 'soft'), referring to the plant's abundant**
mucilage, which sounds gross but is undeniably good in the
context of the toastable sweet that shares its name. The
root of the plant, which is native to the UK, also contains
a useful skin-softening component, and has long been used
for that purpose.

You can grow your own mallow or forage the plant, which
prefers damp conditions near streams and rivers. It has
roundish, soft, lobed leaves that are densely covered in hairs,
but is best distinguished by the pale flowers that appear in
late summer.

Make your hand cream by taking 30 grams of marshmallow
root and placing it in a bowl, then pour over 150 millilitres of
water and leave overnight. The next day, strain the mixture
and measure out 15 millilitres of the concoction. Add in 30
grams of ground almonds, one teaspoon of milk and the same
of cider vinegar, then beat together until the mixture is well
blended. Put into a screw-top jar and keep in the fridge.
Use within one week.

a.

b.

c.

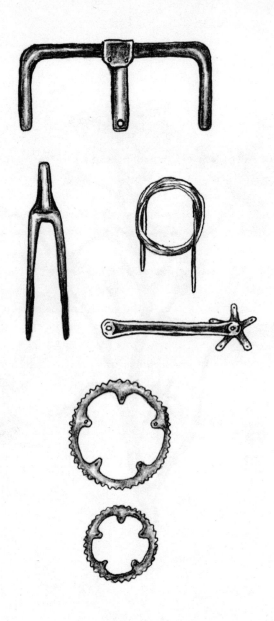

33.
Bike shed

If the bike is the method and the road the medium, then the shed is the spiritual home of the bike. A serious cyclist's shed is a kind of private museum, home to physical objects – but also a psychic archive for treasured memories. Like that time you drank a tequila halfway through that race at Alexandra Palace, or the time you went off the front at Herne Hill, only to be caught mere inches from the line.

The shed is also, of course, the domain of the collector. Though there are few things more melancholy than the broken bicycle, when hung from hooks and displayed among other elegant machines, or among old magazines and other memorabilia, a bike is both paean and stimulus.

34.
Men's Shed Association

It is still perhaps possible to say generally of men that they often don't talk about their feelings or emotions very well, and that health and wellbeing are sometimes a struggle, especially in retirement.

Enter the shed, or rather the UK Men's Sheds Association (UKMSA), a movement that started in Australia and whose mission is to support community-based non-profit organisations and combat loneliness.

This book is a handy guide to the type of thing a Men's Shed group might do, but if you want to set up your own then work around the interests of your members. As well as the classics, you might want to get involved in community projects – restoring local features, helping maintain parks and green spaces, and building things for schools and libraries.

When starting a Men's Shed group, connect with people who share your vision. Ask local businesses to spread the word to their customers; put posters in shop windows and at your local GP's. Tell the local paper what you are up to – you can even hold a public meeting and discuss your ideas. You should definitely get in contact with the UKMSA to help advertise your project. They can also put you in touch with established Shedders to help inspire you.

Visit https://menssheds.org.uk for more information.

'When starting a Men's Shed group, connect with people who share your vision.'

ARTS
&
CRAFTS

35.
How to make a tool board

Many so-called DIY experts get by with an adjustable spanner. But the woman who wants a job done efficiently will organise her multitude of tools on a board, so there is no unnecessary rummaging.

A 1.8m x 1.2m plywood board is an ideal. With this on a bench, juggle your tools until you are happy with the arrangement; light things should go on the top, heavier on the bottom. Trace round each settled piece with a pen. Then get inventive with wood screws – these will be the hanging pegs. Bodge or make custom hangers for your largest tools.

Don't screw your board directly onto the wall, rather, use wall mounts. After marking the outline of your board on the wall, screw five 12cm x 12cm wood blocks directly onto the wall, one for each corner and one in the middle.

Now mount the empty board onto the wall mounts – a friend is helpful here – before hanging your tools.

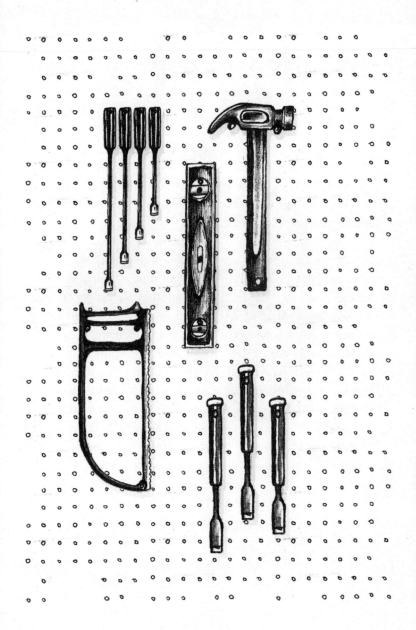

36.
Hand puppets

Hand puppets are a simple and sinister way to teach your children and their friends about conflict between the sexes.

Find a sock to suit – if you are going for social realism then the effect will be enhanced by using old football socks. Find a space for your puppet's face. Put your hand in the sock and identify the upper and lower jaw. You can then draw on the features (as you see them) of your nearest and dearest using a marker pen. Decorate with googly eyes, or metal springs, or comedy ears, or a dog hair wig.

37.
Bike seat lock

The leather bicycle saddle is a rare thing, a valid and unchanging technology around since the earliest days of cycling. They are rare because they get nicked: they are valuable, easy to requisition and difficult to prove ownership of – and everybody wants one. eBay is a thieves' kitchen of Brooks saddles.

The easy and elegant solution is to neatly recycle an old section of bicycle chain and a punctured inner tube, and lock your seat to the frame of your bike.

Clean off the old chain in a shallow bath of petrol. Check how much chain you'll need by running the cleaned length through the mounting rail underneath your saddle and looping it back under one of the seatstays. Break the chain at the desired length – it should be fairly tight – using a chain tool. Wrap the chain in the inner tube, to protect the bike's paint job, and relink the chain.

38.
Carve a clothes hook

Beginner spoon-carvers' first efforts often resemble a withered limb. So why not start your apprenticeship in fine woodworking with a product that's meant to look like this?

Scanning a felled tree will present the apprentice carver with a hundred different potential clothes hooks, with each joint a prospective carving 'blank': this is the very basic, unfinished shape.

Once you have selected and chopped out this blank, split it down the pith (the centre) to get a flat surface, which will eventually go against the wall. Now roughly shape the hook; you should be guided mysteriously and organically by the shape of the blank. Use a large knife or axe and trim it to your tastes, but be sure to leave enough wood so the hook is strong enough to bear the weight of your Barbour.

Now start whittling your hook. Practise essential carving techniques and knife grips learned from Willie Sundqvist's *Swedish Carving Techniques.*

Round out the ends, leaving enough room for mounting screws in the final shape. The beginner will sand down the surface to achieve a final finish, but the wood guru will always finish their carving with the knife.

39.
Tsutsumi

The aesthetic consideration of how something might be revealed suffuses aspects of classical Japanese society. When something is wrapped it becomes precious. If the giver wraps deliberately, then so might the receiver unwrap deliberately: this choreographs a transition of mood. This in turn leads to tsutsumi, or the art of packaging. Embracing this will bring added value to those last-minute gifts, such as a chocolate orange.

Perhaps the simplest way is through 'flower wrapping', where you use a rubber band to create a corsage-style bow on top of your gift. Use a printed furoshiki wrapping cloth and place your gift in the middle. Pull the right and left corners into the middle, followed by the top and bottom corners. Tie them with a rubber band. Then pull the longer (so top and bottom) ends through the rubber again to create a flower shape.

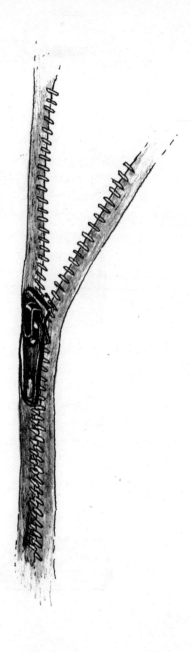

Shedonism

40.

Sew a purse

We all love a rough-look leather item, something well-worn that reminds us both of the craftsmanship and the cow, whether battered shoes or the purse you find here. You won't need specialist skills but you will be using a sewing machine.

Mark out two rectangles (14cm x 11cm is about right) on the wrong side of a piece of leather hide, using a ruler and a biro. Cut out the two shapes using good scissors. You will also need a couple of small tabs (3.5cm x 2cm), used to attach the zipper.

Fold these tabs neatly around a zipper (10cm) and clamp with mini bulldog clips. Using your machine, sew these in place. Use a large-ish stitch length for a nice visible finish.

Take your zipper and sit it upside down along one of the long sides, on the finished side of your leather, right up against the edge. This might seem odd, but you will be folding it all back over. Stitch as close to the teeth as possible. Now topstitch along the edge of the leather you have just sewn. This will hold it in place and provide a neat, professional finish. Do the same with the other piece of leather.

Fold it all back together, secure with bulldog clips, and – with the zip undone – start stitching all around the edges, starting at the top edge. Trim what's left around your sewing, as neatly as you like, and turn your purse the right way out through the open zipper.

41.
Emboss
leather goods

Embossed leather goods are a short cut to a first-class frame of mind. For this cool and hands-on process you'll only need a few bits.

You'll need an embossing stamp: send off for one of your own design, perhaps a fantasy family crest, so a minidigger or twin corn on the cob. And a sturdy cylinder to hold it. This 'hammering handle' will need to be strong enough to withstand regular bashing.

Before bashing, use a damp sponge to moisten your leather item. This will soften it, and make it easier to manipulate. Then affix the leather to a sturdy surface using C-clamps.

Place your stamp on the surface of the leather, then, holding it in place with a strong grip, use a mallet to pound your design into place.

42.

Photographic darkroom

If working with 35mm film is more meditative than using a phone camera, requiring more thought than a digital point and shoot, then developing a film is a way of seeing the past come magically to life. To do this, you will need a shed that is totally dark.

Darkroom equipment is less expensive and more widely available than it used to be, because many people are chucking out enlargers and other paraphernalia. You can also get second-hand trays, film tanks and measuring cylinders, but make sure they are in good condition.

Every darkroom has distinct wet and dry areas. In the dry part of your shed, set up your enlarger with a lens and multi-grade filters. In the wet area, set up three trays – for the developer, stop bath and fixer. The shed needn't have running water, as you can always fill a bucket for washing off prints.

43.
Axe block

The axe block, like the rough mallet, is a symbol of what some have called 'the new wood culture'. This is for resting your clothes hook or perhaps your wooden spoon on when you are doing the initial chopping strokes with an axe. The block reflects the energy that an axe throws into it, so all of the force comes back into whatever you are working on.

It doesn't matter what sort of wood you use, but if you use a softer type your axe will stick, like a dart in a dartboard. It shouldn't wobble and needs to be a sensible height (between 40 and 50 centimetres), and around 30 to 35 centimetres in diameter. You can slightly sculpt the block by angling it towards you or adding a notch or a hollow to support your work.

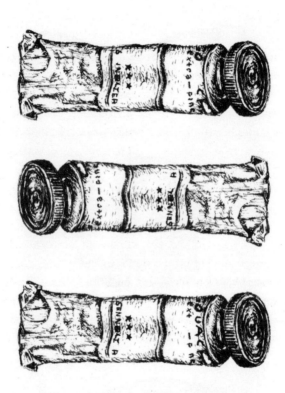

44.
Artist's studio

The artist's studio shed may be a home for the correct paraphernalia – sketchbooks, watercolour tubes, pens and brushes – and a discreet space away from domestic routine. Or a space for creative chaos, surrounded by clutter – spoons, number plates, vegetables, obsolete televisions – in which your art emerges from an unlikely combination of personal effects.

The shed lends itself to the still life. Let your objects choose you, then you can circle them (as one still-life artist has suggested) 'like prey'. Painting should not be rushed, and might be returned to from time to time as the day goes by. Bring your objects to life with thoughtful lighting. Music can move you in a subliminal way that becomes visible in the painting. Aim to reach a state where you are not totally conscious of what you're doing.

45.
Lino print

The lino print might seem very humble, but here you will be following in the footsteps of artists including the Russian Constructivists and Picasso.

You'll need a basic lino-cutting tool with a plastic handle which can hold various shapes of blade. Differently shaped blades produce different cuts, so sacrifice a piece of lino to get a feel for what you can do. Try straight lines and curved, short and long, stabs and jerks, hatching and cross-hatching. You should of course remember that what you cut away will not be printed – it's what's left behind that counts.

Some will opt for the fine control that traditional lino offers, while others may prefer softer, specialist printmaking lino, for the ease of cutting curved lines. Once you've cut your lino into your chosen pattern, spread a thin layer of printing ink (stickier than paint) evenly across the surface, using a brush or a rolling tool. Then lay a sheet of textured paper over it and apply pressure to the back of the paper using smooth, circular movements, before peeling away.

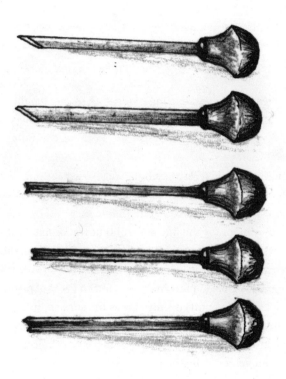

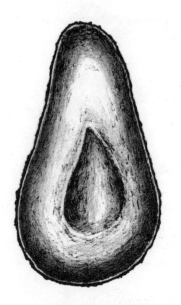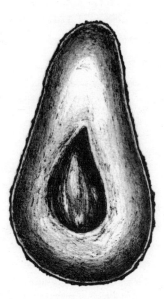

46.
Natural dye

If you are (or you know) a knitter then it is worth dyeing your own wool. Using natural plant dye adds an alchemical element to a craft process, and as described here it is very low-tech.

No two batches will be the same and you can employ a huge variety of plants, from eucalyptus to dried dahlias. This recipe uses the humble avocado, as a way to produce an unlikely but beautiful soft pink shade.

Save avocado skins and stones – or ask for waste from your local hipster café – removing any remaining flesh and allowing them to dry fully. Add several handfuls to a large stainless-steel pan, then cover with two to three times as much water. Bring to the boil on a stove and simmer. Meanwhile, soak natural wool so that it's wet enough to take the dye readily. After an hour, wring out the wool.

Strain the dye into a bowl, then return the liquid to the pan and allow it to cool slightly. Now add your wool, swirling it around so it sits evenly, and return to the heat, bringing it briefly to the boil. Then let it simmer for around an hour. When the wool reaches the desired shade, lift it out and hang it up to dry.

'Down the centuries, the finest scientific minds have scratched their heads over the camera obscura effect.'

47.
Making a camera obscura

Down the centuries, the finest scientific minds – from Greece to China – have scratched their heads over the camera obscura effect, which is that an image projected through a pinhole is inverted or reversed. This is something you too can easily puzzle over in your shed.

The simplest way is to cover the shed window with thick curtains, leaving a small gap to place a toilet roll between them as a tunnel for the light from outside. Your shed needs to be truly dark; the brighter it is outside, the better the effect will be. If the light is adequate, an image of the scene beyond your toilet roll will be projected naturally (but upside down) onto the wall of your shed. You can enhance the effect by hanging a white sheet on the projecting wall.

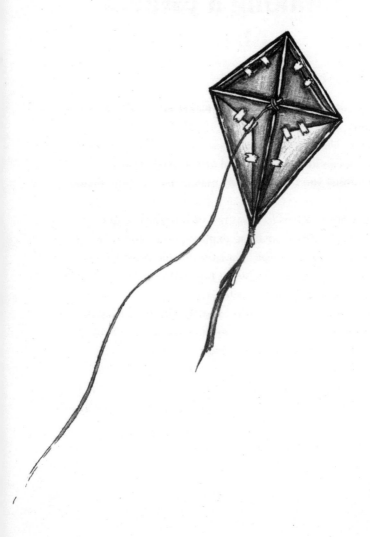

48.
Make a kite

For this simple kite, fold a broadsheet newspaper to create a square, then cut this out.

Then cut two lengths of bamboo or balsa wood dowel. The longer piece should run the full diagonal length of your square – this is the spine. Also cut a shorter cross spar, to sit about two thirds of the way up the spine. Secure these rods together with string to form a cross, and tape them securely to the paper. Add four other rods to create an exterior diamond. Secure these to the paper and fold the edges over to lock it all in place.

Now create the 'keel' (or anchor) for the string you will use to fly the kite. Make four holes in the taped section – two on each side of the central cross – and feed a string through both sets to make a little loop.

Use a strip of cloth to make a tail – this helps the kite fly with added stability. Finally, tie a long flying string to the keel loops.

49.

Tote bag

After you have worn your jeans to death, prove your commitment to the post-plastic age by making this neat tote bag. This is possible even if your sewing skills are limited, as a few slip-ups will only add to its rustic charm.

First, cut two fabric rectangles of equal size out of your old jeans. Roughly mark out where you're going to attach your handles, about a third of the way down the bag.

Hem the top edges by laying out the (unfolded) rectangles, so that the wrong side (i.e. the inside of the jeans) is facing up. Fold just the top edge of the fabric down by an inch and run an iron along its edge to create a crease. Using a sewing machine, or stitching by hand, make a straight stitch half an inch (1.3cm) below the folded edge of the fabric. Repeat on the other rectangle.

Now place the hemmed rectangles back-to-back so the wrong side of the fabric is facing out. Sew along the sides and bottom, again using a straight stitch.

For the handles, cut two strips of equal length (you can make these as long or as short as you like) and 5 centimetres in width. Fold each in half so the inside of the fabric faces outward. Use an iron to crease the fold. Make a straight stitch along the long edges of both handles. Turn the handles right side out by feeding a wire or an unbent coat hanger through the tube, and stitch these onto the bag. Finally turn the whole thing the right way out.

50.
Screen printing

To make your own screen, buy some mesh and the kind of cheap frame used for stretching canvas. Pull the mesh over the frame so it is drum-taut, and staple it evenly around the edges.

Start with a simple design sketched onto plain paper, then cut it out to create a stencil. Lay your T-shirt on a flat surface and place the stencil where you want the image to appear. Now put your screen carefully on top. Put a tablespoon of fabric screen-printing ink in a line at the top edge of your screen. Holding the screen down firmly with your hand, place a squeegee above the ink and, applying some pressure, pull it down the screen. Repeat. Lift the screen from the bottom edge and away.

51.
Sharpening knives

Whetstones are the best way to keep your knives sharp. This means using a series of graded stones, a little like sandpapers. These are water stones, so you need to 'activate' them by soaking them in water for a few minutes prior to use. Keep them damp while you're sharpening by splashing a bit more water on every now and again.

Mark the blunt edge of the blade with a coloured marker. Then, with the knife pressed flat, make a few passes over the coarsest stone – this will be about a 180 grade – from tip to the heel; the marked edge will allow you to see what you've missed. Don't push down excessively, rather go lightly and let the stone do the work.

Working one side and then the other will develop a microscopic 'burr' or overlap, where the metal – which is softer than you think – curls over. Moving through the graded stones will allow you to clean this up. Head up towards 1000 grade, which is really a polishing stone and will produce a very sharp edge.

52.
Tile tabletop

If you are a habitual boot-fair or flea-market rummager then you will no doubt have seen a stack of beautiful vintage tiles for sale – beautiful, but not plentiful enough to do anything practical with. Or so you thought.

One way of rescuing a battered old table is to make it tile-topped. You will need a wooden table top (although you can always lay a plywood board on top of glass). Simply arrange your tiles on this top first – this is a dry run – to get an accurate pattern. Cutting tiles with a tile cutter is not difficult, but use eye protection.

Now remove the tiles and spread adhesive on the board with a trowel. Add your tiles on top. Let this sit overnight – or better, for 24 hours – before grouting. This can be hell on the hands, so wear gloves. Use a rubber float to get the grout in between the tiles, and wipe off any excess with a damp sponge immediately.

53.
Rope basket

The plastic bag is gone, and if you consider the tote passé then why not also try making this coiled rope basket, perfect for garden cuttings or the fruits of your foraging.

Set your sewing machine to its widest, longest zigzag stitch. In addition to a #16 needle and some good-quality polyester thread, you'll need around 36 metres of $^3/_{16}$-inch rope (a well-used poly-cotton clothes line will be perfect) and the patience of a Shinto deity.

To begin, fold about 5 centimetres of the end of the rope in half (start your sewing at the fold), and keep the working end (the rest of the rope) on the right-hand side. Sew the fold together using a zigzag stitch, making sure you are hitting both sections of rope with your needle. Once you reach the end, turn the corner, and sew along this new section. Keep repeating this doubling back, at ever longer lengths: this way your bag is always expanding. At the ends, leave the needle down and raise the presser foot to pivot around. From there, just keep adding rope and sewing around the edge.

54.
Sky lantern

The invention of the sky lantern is attributed to the military strategist Zhuge Liang (181–234 AD), who is said to have used a message-laden sky lantern to summon help when he was surrounded by enemy troops.

Sky lanterns are best made using rice or parchment paper, as these have good tensile strength – which prevents the paper from tearing – and are easy to handle. You will need five sheets.

Make a gently funnelling box out of tapered rectangles. These should be about 50cm x 75cm. Stick it all together with glue. Make a square with a final sheet of paper and stick this on the top. Make sure everything is well glued, so the hot air cannot escape.

Use a bamboo strip to create a ring with a circumference equal to the perimeter of the open end of the balloon. Stick this to the rim.

Homemade fuel may sound deadly but you can make this by soaking a folded napkin in molten wax. Create a mesh of fine wire across the open end of the balloon, and also wire on your fuel napkin. Now make streamer-stabilisers and glue these onto the open end to aid balance in the wind.

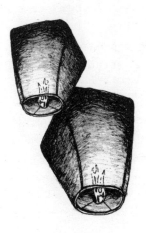

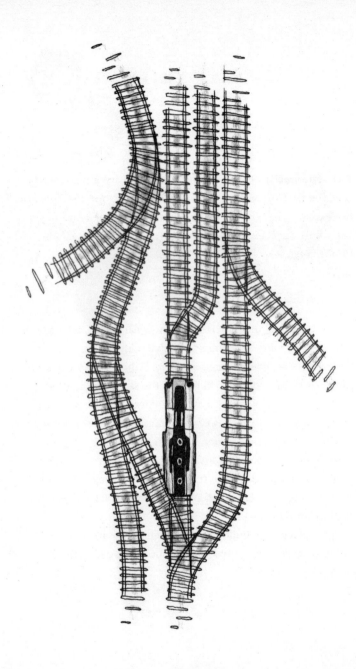

Shedonism

55.
Model railway

The difference between a model railway and a train set is that the first is for adults and the second is for children. In both cases you become overlord of everything from power supply to weather, and – in the privacy of your shed – a kind of god.

Funnily enough, the factors that blight the running of our railways at large also affect the miniaturised version. Ice and sub-zero or even just low temperatures can wreak havoc with your shed's Flying Scotsman, so install a layer of insulation on the inner walls, floor and roof of the shed before you start. Having a ventilation fan will help in the summer months.

Unless you're planning a Hornby–Jurassic Park fantasy hybrid, block up any holes to stop animals and birds getting in.

Some miniaturists prefer nostalgia, recreating a line, branch line or depot they know. Others make it up in their head. Either way, draw the track onto a base board first to ensure it fits, then lay down and secure the track, which can be glued or nailed – or both.

Next place your buildings, and then add 'static grass', which is made of short nylon-type fibres charged with static electricity.

56.
Make a wicker bike basket

If the bicycle is a symbol of freedom, then the bike basket is a sign of halcyon simplicity – somewhere to put your piglets on the way home from the market of your dreams. Even in the real world, this thrifty addition to your sturdy town bike will raise a smile from everybody in the neighbourhood. A trawl of any car boot sale will likely turn up the small picnic basket and old belts that you need.

Roughly secure the basket to your handlebars with two zip ties, threading them through the basket either side of the handlebar stem. Mark a line where the zip tie threads through the basket, and cut a hole wide enough for your belt; you can fix any damaged wicker using wood glue. Use a woven belt – or take a drill bit to a couple of standard belts to make extra holes – so you can get your basket tight to the handlebars.

57.
Slab building a mug

This may sound like a cockney insult but it's an easy way to produce rustic homemade pottery in your shed. An established kiln-sharing scene, nationwide, will help you to fire your pottery.

Roll a quarter of a kilogram of clay into a slab of even thickness (about 6 millimetres). Gently impress a jar (this should be roughly the size of your desired mug) into a corner of the clay. Using the potter's needle or a fettling knife, cut out this circular base.

Determine how tall you want your mug to be, then use a ruler to cut out a rectangle from the middle of your slab: the long sides should equal the mug's circumference and the short sides should equal the mug's desired height.

Now 'weld' it all together. It's best to use a process called slipping and scoring – so score fine, cross-hatched grooves in both clay surfaces that are to be joined, then moisten these grooves with a brush and water before joining the two pieces together.

Create a basic handle the same thickness as before. Weld this firmly to the mug's wall. Mug handles are put to heavy use, so make sure your joints are strong. Generally, slab-built rims need rounding out to be comfortable against the drinker's lips, so work carefully before firing and decorating.

'Made from the plastic bags you always wish you didn't need, this natty lampshade will be a symbol of your guilt.'

58.

Plastic bag lampshade

**Made from the plastic bags you always wish you didn't
need, this natty lampshade will be a symbol of your
guilt, but also a paean to your local grocer, so weirdly
representative of your local milieu. You will become a
sort of Antony Gormley of the corner shop.**

The sculptural element is enhanced if you use slightly thicker
bags, and the same type over and again.

Use an old lampshade as the base for your design. Cut fifty
bags into long strips before rolling these into loose rosettes.
Add a dab of glue to hold the swirl together, before smearing
glue onto the shade too. Press the rosettes into place, so that
you get to see the fineness of the folds. Repeat this as many
times as required and aim for a tightly packed finish.

59.
Make a mallet

The mallet of the modern woodworker is not the same as the ubiquitous comedy or cartoon mallet, but rather a crudely adapted lump from your firewood pile. Think 'club', and you will be near to the mark. This tool will be useful for all of your woodworking.

When choosing your material, go for a wood with reasonably high tensile strength; ash or hazel is best. Choose a bit of wood with a 'knot' or imperfection in it, as these do not split easily.

Choose a length that is easy to swing, and heavy enough to provide force and momentum, but also a handy size to pick up off the floor. The diameter of the hitting end should be wide enough for it to stand up independently. Carve the mallet down to a gradual taper, with the other end just big enough for your hand.

60.
Cardboard box speaker

If (as this book advises) you are to spend more time in your shed, then music should be a part of your plan. This simple cardboard-box speaker is both portable and sustainable. For optimal sound, the small driver unit should be of the best quality you can afford.

You need a heavy-duty cardboard box – corrugated cardboard is better than single-ply; smaller boxes tend to have more structural rigidity, so err on the small side. If you're using a speaker smaller than 15 centimetres across, use a box that is roughly a 20-centimetre cube.

Cut an opening in the side that is large enough for the speaker. Reinforce this wall with another piece of cardboard the same size, with an identical cut-out, and glue this in behind. In fact, if you reinforce with several such sheets your small driver unit will seal quite well. This will improve the sound dramatically, with much more midrange balance.

Poke a tiny hole near the bottom of the side of the box opposite the speaker opening and thread a piece of speaker wire through it.

Mount your speaker into the opening, with bolts and nuts driven through the cardboard wall of the box, and connect the speaker wire to the terminals of the speaker. Close the box and seal it with duct tape. To strengthen the box, you can also reinforce the corners with duct tape.

61.
Model village

The shed model village is the ideal retreat for those wishing to reinstate the past – or perhaps an idealised version of the present – setting out a solid vision of what village life might look like at a time of rapid change.

This is your chance to reopen the post office, or the grammar school, or add CCTV networks and a Polish deli as you see fit. Neat one-sheet plans for models are widely available, and an easy place to start your empire. You will be in good company: aficionados include the artist Rachel Whiteread. Countless inspiring attractions exist around the UK, from Babbacombe to Anglesey.

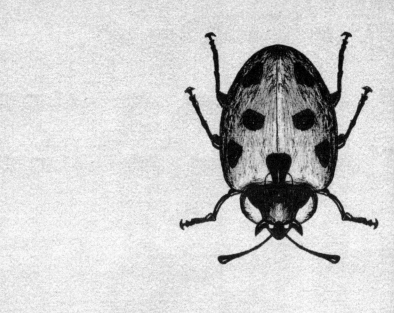

SCIENCE
&
NATURE

62.
Build a bat box

It is perhaps easy to be cynical about any species that you can adopt for charity. Yet bats are a vital indicator species, and changes to their populations are a measure of ecological health at a time when we are busy decimating our natural environment. In the past 50 years, we in the UK have destroyed well over half of our biodiversity.

A bat box should be made from untreated wood, i.e. wood that has not been pressure-treated with chemicals: bats are sensitive to smells, and preservative chemicals may be harmful to them. Make sure your box is made from rough-sawn wood (rather than smooth, planed material) so the bats can get a grip. You also need good, snug joints, as bats hate a draught.

Create a narrow horizontal slit at the back of the box, on the bottom, with a rough piece of wood leading up to it, so that they can clamber up. The ideal bat box has two or more internal compartments, and it's best to make the box as large as possible. A deep cavern makes bats feel safe and keeps the temperature consistent.

63.
Pigeon racing

Pigeon racing has slipped off the radar in recent years, and for this reason it's surely not long before it becomes a hipster pastime.

When turning your shed into a pigeon loft , bear in mind that the average number of birds in a UK loft is 60. And that you also have to create space for the birds to enjoy the sunshine and bathe, as pigeons love a bath. Ensure stable day and night temperatures with a thermostat-controlled unit, and include perches, nest boxes, water troughs and food trays.

Fanciers should exercise their birds around the loft for a minimum of one hour every day. This is in preparation for the day you will pack your pigeons into a low-loader, with all the other birds from your club (there are 2,500 pigeon racing clubs in the UK), before they are driven away and 'liberated' at a far-flung site – up to 620 miles away, possibly in France. This is a race, so use a pigeon clock to record the times of the homecoming.

64.
Mounting butterflies

Mounting butterflies is poor man's taxidermy, and a fitting honour for a recently expired insect. The framed creatures will lend a morbid Victorian glamour to any room.

After dying, a butterfly dries out and will become too brittle to mount, so rehydrate it with relaxing fluid, in a sealed container. This makes the creature sufficiently malleable that you can then pin it through the abdomen, mounting it in your chosen case or cabinet. Be careful not to touch precious, fragile wings with your hands, so use forceps or tweezers to manipulate them into place. Artfully pin the wings down behind the larger veins.

65.
Make a squirrel trap

Grey squirrels get a lot of bad press, as an invasive bully species that has pushed our native red to the margins of existence. They're also a sure sign of urban malaise (*see* pigeon racing, p. 145). Stories have emerged in recent years of squirrels high on crack cocaine. Squirrels chew through electrical wires in lofts, causing fires.

This easy-to-make trap will assure your vigilante revenge. What you do with the squirrel after you have captured it is up to you.

The body of the trap will be made from a length of PVC pipe, around 60 centimetres long and 10 centimetres in diameter. Cut another length of pipe, this time around 10 centimetres long, and fashion a section that slips onto the main body, serving as a pivot. Attach a shortish pencil to this, to serve as a fulcrum. Set this all on a wooden base, with the fulcrum set between two wooden blocks.

Put a cap on one end of the pipe. The other end – the business end – needs to be hinged, to act as a door. Take a bi-fold or 'T' hinge and glue this onto a suitably sized piece of metal cut from a cheap pan. Clamp this on with a hose clamp. Put a piece of coat hanger on the front of the mounting board so it just holds the door up. Smear peanut butter in the tube and wait. When the squirrel goes in, the tube will tip, and the door will close.

'A roof will also serve as a thermal layer to protect your toes while you produce a dance record.'

66.
A living roof

A living roof on your shed is a neat way to increase the planting area in your garden, and provide extra habitat for insects, birds and other creatures. A roof will also serve as a thermal layer to protect your toes while you produce a dance record (*see* p. 192) or brew your own beer (*see* p. 33).

First, make a wooden frame to fit over your shed roof. It needs to be 20–30 centimetres deep to accommodate liners, soil and plants. Ensure there is a gap between the edge of the frame and the shed roof, to allow for drainage of water.

Line the frame with a waterproof sheet; a rubber pond liner will do. Put a moisture-blanket made from woolly fleece on top, and finish this off with a filter sheet – like the sheet you use under a patio to keep weeds out – which will hold fine soils but allow water to pass through.

Add a 4-centimetre layer of expanded clay granules on top of the liners; this is a light substrate in which your plants will grow. Finish with a 4-centimetre layer of a mixture of top soil (70 per cent) and sand (30 per cent).

In some respects, the most interesting way to colonise your roof isn't to plant it at all, but rather to allow seeds to be blown in by the wind or dropped by wildlife. But if you do want to start the roof off, sedum (stonecrop), which attracts bees and butterflies, is hardy and low-maintenance.

67.
Bird-watching hide

The bird enthusiast represents a core trait of Britishness: an obsessive interest in nature. Wannabe W. H. Hudsons have taken part in the RSPB's Big Garden Birdwatch for 40 years.

What better use for your shed than to double it up as a bird-watching hide. Simply cut a rectangle, or remove a couple of lengthways slats, to provide your viewing window. Make sure this is wide enough for you to poke a camera lens through, as the lens is a symbol of your seriousness.

Install a couple of shelves under the window inside, upon which to rest the all-important cups of tea. If you want to go very rustic, then re-wild your shed and garden at the same time, spattering the outside with mud, peat, sharp sand and cement.

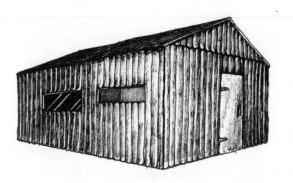

68.
Aquarium

**Aquariums are attractive and it's quite decadent to have
more than one tank. But if you are drawn to expand then
use large tanks, at least 60 centimetres deep, because
larger bodies of water are more stable than smaller ones,
and enable you to keep more fish. Most fish are also
happier in groups.**

Keeping fish properly involves building complex ecosystems
that harness useful bacteria to recycle waste products. This
takes time to achieve: new tanks may take six weeks or more
to mature, and don't put too many fish in during this period.

Without regular upkeep, an aquarium can quickly turn
into an algae-filled swamp, so set aside time every day for the
various maintenance tasks, such as checking the equipment
and topping up evaporation losses.

Most tropical fish are adapted to a wild environment and
are to a degree chameleonic, so decorate with muted colours
like browns, greys and greens. If you use bright blue gravel
with a catfish, it will turn a sickly pale colour in a futile
attempt to blend in.

Consider stocking platies and danios, which may be
hardier than goldfish. That said, you don't have to stick with
boring fish in the long term, and an understanding retailer will
also often part-exchange if you wish to upgrade to discus or
Malawi cichlids.

69.
Making a fishing fly

If you're an angler, your shed is likely already a repository for your fishing gear, but why not add a craft element with a small workbench and vice – dedicated to the humble act of making imitation insects. Tying your own fly is an intimate art which will only increase your sense of cunning in the long run, having outwitted the fish with a lure of your own creation.

Scissors are the most utilised hand tool on a fly tier's bench. Slim pliers and a dubbing needle are also handy for precise wrapping and poking.

To create the Mohair Leech, you will need a long streamer hook, 140-denier thread, marabou feathers and mohair yarn. Make a few wraps of heavy wire on the hook shank to add weight, or omit weight to create a fly that hovers in the water. Tie a shaggy body out of mohair, picking up a few loose strands to create a dishevelled look, then wind on your feather tail. Tie this simple pattern in black, olive and purple, and you'll quickly be catching.

70.
Herb spiral

Permaculture is a set of ecological design principles centred around whole systems thinking – a kind of osteopathy for the garden – which utilises the patterns and features found in natural ecosystems. The herb spiral is the perfect place to see – and demonstrate – the principles of permaculture at work. While not technically something that you will put in your shed, much of the building and planning elements are best done in a dedicated space.

This is basically a rockery designed to make the most out of the differing light and shade conditions, and different temperatures, you can create in your garden. Different plants have different needs, and by creating a spiral that is raised in the centre, spiralling down to ground level, lots of microclimates are created, some sunny and moist – for plants like basil – and some cooler – for plants like parsley – thereby catering to a range of species.

Plan out a 2-metre diameter spiral – this should be enough space to wind around a couple of times. Start with a cone of soil and rubble about 60 centimetres high. Then lay out the spiral design with whatever material is on hand, so stones, old bricks or bottles. Add soil in varied ways to provide weed protection, compost fertilising, moisture retention and air.

When planting the spiral, consider how each plant might affect the rest of the spiral, as some herbs don't like each other.

Consider putting a small pond near where the spiral spills out onto the ground. This will provide a good habitat for the frogs which will keep the area pest-free. It's also a good water source for plants like mint, which love water.

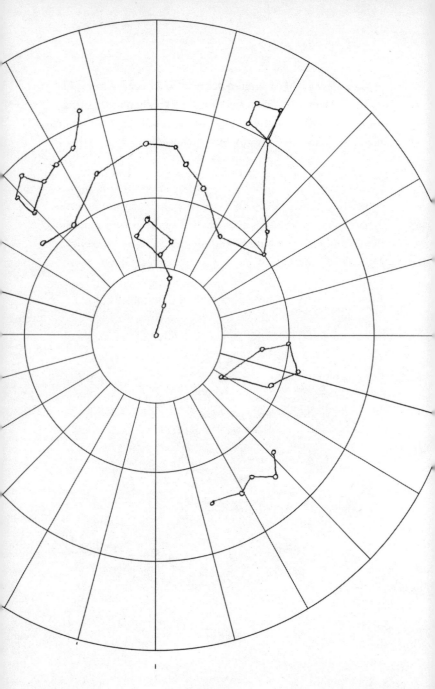

Shedonism

71.
Home observatory

**The stargazing community may pray firstly for clear skies –
generally, the best time for stargazing is when the moon is
in a crescent or gibbous phase – and it's best to get to know
the galaxy with binoculars and an old-fashioned chart.**

Technology, however, allows us a deeper glimpse into space,
and the modern astronomer will build a split shed, with a
'warm room' for computers (used for processing images),
and an open area for your powerful telescope. You may wish
to engineer your shed roof, so the open area is cunningly
exposed by a roof segment that rolls away, on supported rails.

72.
Beekeeping log

The most ancient beekeeping likely involved adapting a hollow tree: the earliest recorded log hive was found in Switzerland, circa 3380 BC. You can recreate this primitive husbandry by suspending a chopped log from a tree, or by propping it up.

Typically your log should be around 1.5 metres long, with a girth of about 60 centimetres. You will need to clean it up before tempting the bees. Firstly use fire to hollow out the log. Start by drilling a hole right through the length of the log, starting at one end, with a long drill bit. Then prop it up at an angle and light a small fire at the base. You can direct the flames into the hole, and speed up the burn, by blowing air around tactically with a length of pipe.

Fashion bespoke, removable boards to snugly seal up the ends. Insert two hazel 'spales' – these are basically cross-hatched sticks – fixed horizontally within the log to help support the growing comb. (When harvesting, only take your honeycomb from around the sides as the centre belongs to the bees.) Now drill three entrance holes near the base of the log, and bait the interior with old comb, wax and propolis (bee glue). These incentives should ensure that a local swarm find it pretty quickly.

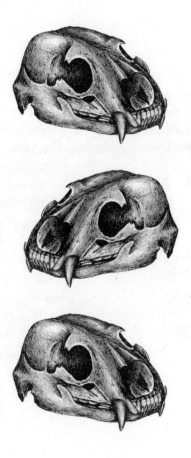

73.
Preserve a skull

Most people recoil when faced with a skull. Yet there is something to be found in the contemplation of this bone cage, as Hamlet knew; as Giacometti knew. Preparing a found animal skull yourself will only enhance meditation. The shed is a good spot for this dirty deed.

First you have to find your lucky critter. A day in the countryside will turn up a decomposing sheep or badger – we've all seen them. (Fresh kills are full of unspeakable parasites and it is not recommended to take dead animals from the road.) Look out for something that has been gone a long time.

Mother Nature might have stripped the head of lingering flesh, but you may still want to clean it up with a toothbrush. The purist will stop at this; the ornamentalist will whiten the bones with a dilute concentration of hydrogen peroxide. You can glue in any teeth that fell out during the process, and fix the jawbone with hot glue if necessary, before sitting your skull on the collected works of Samuel Beckett.

74.

Aquaponics

Aquaponics is the combination of aquaculture (growing fish for food) and hydroponics (growing food without soil), and is a self-sustaining closed-loop system well suited to the shed. For this project, imagine a terrace arrangement, with a grow bed on top and a fish pond of sorts on the bottom.

At the heart is a pump which takes water from the pond and brings it up onto your edible plants. The method is completely organic, using fish waste to grow the plants, and reduces the amount of water needed to grow your veg.

Leafy greens, tomatoes and peppers are popular choices. The most common fish that people use are tilapia. For the fish house you can improvise, with barrels, bath tubs, large food containers, or anything else with a waterproof liner. You will need a water pump to get the pond water up into the grow bed, and a siphon to then drain it. You will also need a sump to ensure the fish tank remains full throughout.

Your grow bed should be the same size as your pond. So salvage another water-tight container for your plants, and build a stand to sit the bed above the tank. Add a grow medium to your bed. This replaces the need for soil; the most popular choice is clay pebbles. These provide an excellent surface for roots to grow into and are also pH-neutral, so won't affect your water supply.

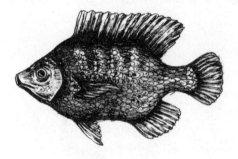

Shedonism

75.

Wormery

Ensure a steady supply of superb fertiliser by employing worms to work for you. You will need to build them a house. This will live outside in the summer but is best brought into your shed when the weather gets frosty.

It is best to construct a wormery out of a large wooden box, with a wooden lid. Worms need air, so use a 12mm bit to drill enough holes in the base to ensure good airflow. Also add small holes to the lid and at the top of the sides.

Cover the bottom with a sheet of newspaper, so the worms don't fall out. Add about half a bucket of worm bedding, i.e. compost. This will help the worms feel at home.

Then add worms. You can buy them online or from a fishing tackle shop, and you'll need about 300 to start. Add food, little and often to begin with: teabags, banana skins, vegetable peelings and coffee grounds are all good; onion skins, citrus and very spicy or oily foods are not. Your wormery should always be about two-thirds carbon-rich matter, so top up with cardboard, newspaper or woodchips.

Cover the surface of the worms – any cardboard, newspaper or even an old towel will do. Then cover with the lid. In summer, place the wormery on bricks in a sheltered spot, away from direct sunlight.

76.
Bug house

Leaving areas of your garden messy and untended may be anathema to some, but providing an insect habitat in the form of a homemade bug house will ensure effective pollination of your garden plants. Bugs also help to strip your plants of unwanted aphids.

A vast number of invertebrates – including spiders, ladybirds, lonely bees and beetle larvae – will find the wood and plant-stem tunnels here irresistible, and quickly make nests or hibernate in winter.

Make your bug house from solid wood. Cut the sides to size using a saw and glue the pieces together first, before screwing the whole box together. Hunt down suitable twigs from the garden, then arrange within the structure, packing them tightly so it all stays put, but ensuring there are lots of crevices for the bugs.

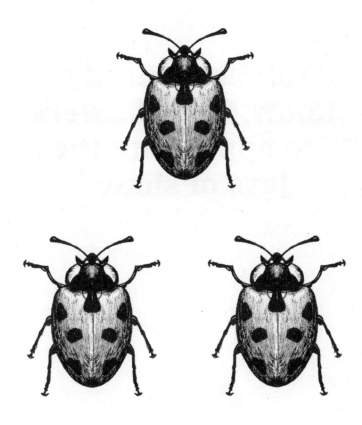

'You don't need to know *Ghostbusters* to appreciate the joys of slime.'

77.
Making slime

You don't need to know *Ghostbusters* to appreciate the joys of slime, which can be made at home. Slime is best made when assisted by kids, who will enjoy the process as much as the play afterwards.

Pour 2 cups of lukewarm water into a medium-sized pot. Add 1 tablespoon of organic natural fibre – a gungy food supplement – and 1 teaspoon of corn flour, then 3–4 drops of natural food colouring. Gently stir to combine. Place the whole on medium–low heat and boil for 5 minutes, but do not stir.

78.
Drying wood

The log pile is a sign of virility in many countries, a conspicuous show of your preparedness, but also of your ordered mind, even your artfulness.

A recent twelve-hour Norwegian TV special was split fifty–fifty on whether it was better to stack logs bark side up or bark side down. Whichever you decide, make sure that there is an air gap behind and in front of the stack, to allow the ends of the logs to breathe.

Dry wood acts like a sponge, so stack it on bearers – these prevent moisture coming up from the bottom of the stack, and can be any old bits of wood, such as fence posts (which contain preservatives) or even old pallets.

THE
MODERN
SHED

Shedonism

79.
Shed library

Rapid change has affected the way we consume the written word. This coupled with the declining number of people using libraries – though library use is still strong in the most deprived areas of the UK – means that the free borrowing of books is seriously at risk.

If your shed is a haven for private reading, then why not also open it up to the public in a radical gesture of community solidarity?

If you are taking precious titles to the shed then install a dehumidifier, as books don't like damp days, or indeed too much natural light.

The Little Free Library movement has really taken off; consider your shed the logical extension of this. Perhaps start with a micro-library (an open box, with weatherproof plastic front) on the wall outside your house, adding a few representative titles such as *The Brothers Karamazov* and Kelly Holmes's autobiography. Leave a comments book inside with a brief instruction to 'Take what you want; swap if you like'. Add a signpost to the main library building out back.

Be aware that there is also a burgeoning 'tool library' scene, and a growing awareness that libraries need not be confined to books, so be creative in what you lend.

80.
Nuclear bunker

Every self-respecting billionaire has a bunker, a feature of conspicuous excess equivalent to having your remains cryogenically frozen. The prototype bunker is visible in most Bond films, replete with shark pools and hordes of fearful ear-muffed minions.

Create the effect of an impending apocalypse by assiduously blocking out all natural light. Then add a window-like high-definition screen to your shed, projecting images of abandoned cornfields, burning skyscrapers or empty cities. Include air- and water-filtration systems, and fit solar and a wind turbine to the roof to take yourself fully off-grid (*see* p. 210). Grow plants and breed tilapia fish for food (*see* aquaponics, p. 166), and set the whole affair off by wearing a tinfoil hat.

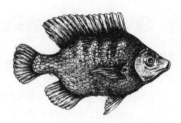

'If you want to get rich
with cryptocurrency
then you should
get a dedicated
crypto-shed.'

81.

Make a fortune in cryptocurrency

If you want to get rich with cryptocurrency (this is essentially money, but underpinned by obscure digital ideas and systems) then you should get a dedicated crypto-shed. This shed will be useful to house the computer hardware you need to mine bitcoin effectively.

Cryptocurrencies like bitcoin depend on something called a blockchain, basically a public transaction ledger that requires dedicated machines to process the complex transactions involved. Back in 2009 you could sort of hire out your desktop computer to help with these transactions – and get paid in bitcoin as a result. But as the value of bitcoin skyrocketed, goggle-eyed miners began to invest in ever-more sophisticated hardware to help them in the hunt for this nebulous lucre. So you'll now need a specialist 'mining rig' – which means a forest of wires and a thatch of space-age hard drives – and, preferably, a large shed. Expect one hell of an electricity bill.

82.
Dog grooming

The pampered pooch is a feature of the modern urban environment, a kind of fluffy ventriloquist's doll. Why not tap in to the expanding pet industry? To get a sense of where we are headed, this is currently worth over $5 billion a year in the US.

You will need a shed to accommodate the basic tools of the trade: so clippers, shears, scissors, brushes, shampoos, conditioners, sprays, dryers and ear-cleaning products, plus shelves to accommodate optional glamour accessories such as bandanas and bows.

83.

Online trading

The press is full of stories of small-time traders who have made a success out of selling on eBay and Etsy. Stories also abound ('the rise of the storage unit') of these businesses getting way out of hand, and of people having to take on extra space to squirrel away their excess militaria.

Why not bring the two things together in your shed? The best way is to sell products that you have a feel for, and can source reliably and store. If you are interested in beachcombing for weathered shards of glass, for example, then consider how you might turn this into attractive jewellery.

Don't try to be the cheapest. Do your research on sellers of similar goods and get an idea as to what your product seems to be worth. Look carefully at the costs of selling online: selling fees, final value fees, product costs, postage costs, etc. Customer service is key – a feedback score of less than 90 per cent can really hurt traders – so work on communication with buyers, and use Google's keyword tool to generate natty titles that will show up in search engines.

84.
Coffee shop

You will no doubt have seen small, opportunistic coffee outlets, crammed into the side of existing shops, a house front on a distant tourist trail, and on a station platform. So if you are a coffee lover and your gaff is en route to anywhere, consider opening your own.

The key lies in the bean, so source one locally and have a range of weird words at hand to describe the ephemeral aromas: caramel, umami, acid. You can pick up a fairly major coffee machine second-hand for a few hundred pounds – make this the centrepiece of your business. If you don't want to stretch to this then filter coffee is also back, so employ the trusted drip method to produce some truly vibrational effects.

85.

Create a protest placard

Make your razor sharp wit conspicuous at any one of the current protest marches, with a beautiful placard – a kind of folk art.

This is all about the DIY ethic but do think about using foam boards, which are both rigid and lightweight enough to be hoisted all day. Text-based posters with a limited colour palette have the most impact. Seven words is almost too many. Rough out your design first and make sure that your text fits, because there's nothing worse than having a host of deformed letters crammed into a tiny space at the edge.

That said, don't be afraid to experiment with mixed media to achieve your effects. One memorable placard from the Women's March was a vivid celebration, fringed in red wool.

86.
Produce a dance record

In the olden days – twenty years ago – you would have had to rely on a middleman to field and license your musical creations. Today, the unstoppable rise of the computer and disruptive web technologies means you can feasibly make a hit from the comfort of your shed.

As well as your laptop, you will need a pair of studio monitor speakers and a digital audio workstation, which will give you control of your synthesiser suite. The hard wood interior of your shed will rattle the sound, so get some rugs on the floor and hang the walls with tapestries of Shaun Ryder. Once you get going, just keep pumping out the tunes, as a frivolous and disposable nature has always been at the heart of the genre.

87.

Casino in a shed

So much of the casino has gone online that, as with the art-house cinema (*see* p. 198), you can collect the physical accoutrements of erstwhile gambling dens for very little cash. With just a few stools and a card table, you can easily recreate the stage set of *A Streetcar Named Desire*.

The interior of your gambling shed should be designed to get your fellow gamblers to play for as long as possible. Aim to confuse them. Traditionally, casinos have forgone windows and clocks, so install a controlled lighting system that makes your shed look and feel the same at 3 a.m. as it does at 3 p.m. Engaging players' senses also keeps them gambling. So get on the fast music, red lights and pleasing aromas (*see* essential oils, p. 60) to increase profits.

88.
Vlogging

Vlogging is a fact, if not a word, with some online diarists taking home a reputed £50,000 per month. To be a successful vlogger you will likely have an interest in beauty, lifestyle, fashion or health, though some successful vloggers are harder to define, making films about toilet breaks or travails with the garage door.

The shed is an ideal place to set up your studio and host your film and editing tools. Vlog pioneers recommend full editorial control, so learn to use Final Cut Pro or similar in your shed.

Don't make things look too perfect, as viewers like a rough diamond and want to see your human side. Trash-talking might make you popular in the short term, but if you are looking for brand tie-ins then be nice and reach out to businesses. Look to collaborate with other similar artists and set yourself targets – 100,000 YouTube subscribers is currently the magic figure.

89.
Art-house cinema

The tiled art-deco frontages of old cinemas now house cheap furniture stores nationwide, and with people turned off the brash audio and damp seats of the multiplex, there is predictably a move back towards cinema's original intimacies. And how much more intimate can you get than a shed – a six- or ten-seater cinema where you can build community ties (*see* shed library, p. 179) and inflict the most obscure aspects of your personality on your neighbours.

Create the dimmed aura of excitement so crucial to the suspension of belief, the gentle fade of conversation and the muted rustling of popcorn, by adding floor wash lighting, or even a starry sky. So many traditional theatres have folded that there are vintage fittings still in circulation. Plush red cinema seats are key to the effect, and a quick trawl of eBay will reveal a set of three hefty micro-sofas for as little as the price of a cinema ticket.

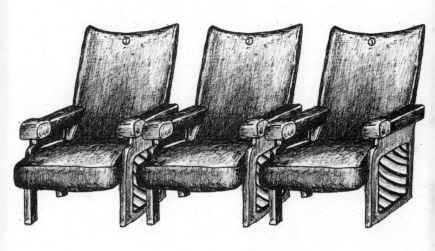

90.
Write a bestseller

The novel is in some respects the epitome of expression, requiring only pen and paper to create. Yet despite rumours of bestselling authors putting together their masterpieces in coffee shops, a safer space is surely essential. And if Virginia Woolf advocated passionately for *A Room of One's Own*, **then we might update this dictum for the space-saving age:** *A Shed of One's Own.*

The only way to improve is to write daily, and habituate the impulses that drove you to consider writing in the first place. Create a time when you are free from other obligations and responsibilities, but follow your metabolism.

Stream of consciousness is a style but it is also a key to freeing up your creativity. Get used to writing whatever comes into your head – but don't go mad.

According to Stephen King:

The most interesting situations can usually be expressed as a What-if question:
What if vampires invaded a small New England village?
(Salem's Lot) . . .
What if a young mother and her son became trapped in their stalled car by a rabid dog? (Cujo)

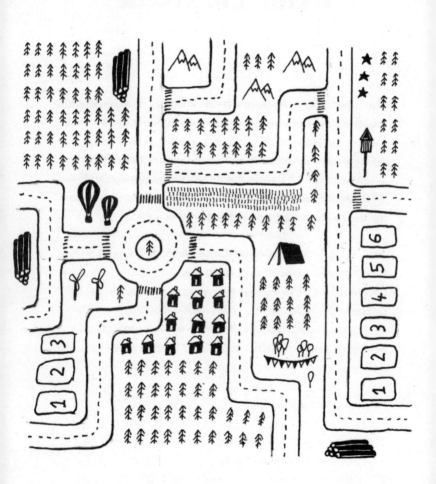

91.
Kids' playroom

The shed can be an escape from domestic travails, but why not flip it and remove your domestic travails to the shed?

Scribblings on your white walls are an inevitable if slightly irritating part of having small children, so why not create a place where they're actually encouraged to do it. A blackboard wall is a fun addition to any playroom.

Make the shed floor a site for the imagination with a road mat, for driving toy cars and trucks around. This will also make your shed feel much cosier.

Giving kids a place to read and relax is as important as lively play, so find a light corner and fill it with accessible books, then make the area inviting with cushions and beanbags.

'Look closely at TVs, microwaves and be ready to tear these down to the main components, and put them back together again before anyone notices.'

92.

Hack the mainframe

Those who flirt with the dark side of the web are known as black hat hackers, locked in battle with the heroic 'white hats' who employ their silky skills to combat the dodgy dealings of the former.

If you have ambitions in either area then you must cultivate an obsessive interest in electronics. Look closely at TVs, microwaves – basically anything with a circuit board – and be ready to tear these down to the main components, and put them back together again before anyone notices.

Then anonymise yourself; the hacker exists at night. Get used to coordinating with other avatars, aiming at a vaguely self-defined goal, focussing primarily on 'lulz'.

The black hat hacker's main tool is the virus, which you write and inject into software so that anyone who uses it will be infected. Once someone opens a malicious email, you'll be notified. Now you have complete control. Sit and wait for the perfect opportunity to spoof your victim's email in the middle of a transaction. Then put the money into a different bank account and change it into untraceable cryptocurrency.

Over time, you will become bored with your anonymity. Becoming a good guy – it's worth it: the demand for high-quality hackers to work for professional companies far outstrips the supply – involves gaining the unlikely-sounding EC-Council Certified Ethical Hacker qualification.

93.
Record shop

The demise of the record shop was announced somewhat prematurely, with vinyl now undergoing a well-publicised renaissance – over 4 million units were sold in the UK in 2018.

The shed is the perfect place to secret yourself away with your collection. But why not go one step further and turn your shed into a mini record store? Having a small store is a strength because you can rotate stock more often. It's also very sociable – 'Three customers at a time please!'

94.
Start a podcast

Podcasts tumble happily into the gaps left by mainstream audio media, allowing the listener to handpick from an ever-increasing host of topics, including feminism, agony aunts and tractors. This also carves out a niche for the home or shed podcaster, which fits well with the growing trend of slow radio: so record a podcast on pencils, or work on an edit of the sound of sheep you recorded in southern Spain.

Sound quality begins with the microphone, so splash out on a decent USB-one that is front-firing, with good noise rejection, so it picks up your voice clearly without unwanted peripheral sounds. If you plan to host guests, then record online calls with simple and inexpensive technology, and edit your work easily with free software. You can upload the finished product to hosting sites like Libsyn, Soundcloud and TuneIn, or aim to get your podcast live on iTunes.

Think about recording a jingle that easily identifies your show. This is best done late at night after watching a horror movie with a bottle of vodka.

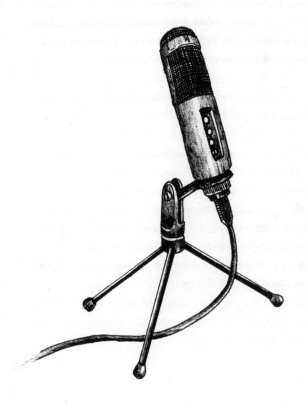

The Modern Shed

95.
Take yourself off-grid

Taking your shed off-grid is feasible, but which method you choose – wind or sun – will be dictated by which part of the UK you live in. Those in the gusty north may be installing a solar folly. So best to hedge your bets – a mix of the two will ensure you have energy year-round.

If you do go for the turbine, positioning is key: the power of wind is proportional to the cube of its speed, so twice the wind speed gives eight times the power. Micro roof-mounted wind turbines are cheap but less efficient (and will produce a lot less electricity) than pole-mounted ones.

It's possible to install small-scale solar for about £100. A rummage at your local hardware store should provide the required combination of solar panel, charge controller, battery, inverter and socket. A 10-watt photovoltaic panel coupled with a 15 Ah battery should provide plenty of juice for endless afternoons of the BBC World Service.

The Modern Shed

96.
Walk-in closet

**If your trucker hat collection is getting out of hand, or
your high heels and halter necks are beginning to rile your
other half, then don't clear the clutter but instead relocate
it to another room – a dedicated space for your clothes,
in your shed.**

When planning your shed wardrobe, first separate your short
and long garments, measuring how many metres of hanging
space you need for each – then add 20 per cent more. A set
of closed cupboards will protect more expensive garments
from dust. To avoid moths, fabrics made from animal hair
such as wool should be stored in sealed boxes, though bear in
mind that cleanliness is the best line of defence, so keep your
clothes shed spick and span. Shoe bars only work with heeled
footwear, so for flats choose shelves and see-through plastic
boxes. These are great for stacking as well as locating the right
shoes at a glance.

    LEDs give the best light for viewing garments. Gucci-wearers
might consider adding a heating unit with a thermostat.

97.
3D printer

While it may not be practically possible to recreate the concrete bridges or recycled plastic chairs at the cutting edge of 3D printing, you could become the neighbourhood go-to girl or guy doing a strong line in replacement knobs for washing machines, or car stereo parts.

It is possible to pick up a 3D printer for around £1,000, but be aware that your first will likely not be your last. You can also buy a printer that is self-replicating and can make a kit out of itself. Get one that uses polylactic acid (PLA), which is a biodegradable plastic made from cornflour or sugar cane.

You will need support, but the online community is huge. Open-source software groups will guide you through the process of designing your model and converting it into a language that the printer can understand.

98.
Live in a shed

Some may view living in a shed as a sign of the apocalypse, others as a kind of life hack and sign of human resilience.

But before you move in – or think about making a few quid as a shed landlord – consider the practicalities. For occasional use, most people can add a sofa bed to their shed for the odd guest night. But your garden room must comply with building regulations if anyone is going to sleep in it regularly, and if it's going to be a long-term thing then you must also apply for planning permission. Bear in mind that you may be required to pay council tax too.

If this sounds like a way of putting you off, then perhaps it is. This whole book is in essence a manifesto for the pottering and the diverted – an extended definition of the shed – and a request that we maintain the shed as a safe place outside our normal routines. It should be a protected zone – a discreet space we can use to compartmentalise our complex lives, which cannot really be boxed apart from when we choose to be boxed.

99.
'Pirate' radio

Perhaps, ultimately, people will tire of choice and agency in music. Once the randy teenage buzz of showing off your latest found tunes has worn off – tunes appropriated from Mali or Bromley-by-Bow – we will surely all crawl back to radio.

The age of the mainstream, however, is over. Listeners are no longer content being funnelled into the standards, and are dissatisfied hearing only things that they know – save this for the nursing home. To those stuck in these streams, music has never changed.

Online-only stations such as NTS have given new contour to the musical landscape, and you too can play your part. You don't need a licence to set up this type of internet radio, though if it adds to your edge to think of your work as 'pirate' then by all means erect a rickety-looking sham-antennae on top of your local tower block. You will however need permissions so consider acquiring licensing through a service such as Live365.com.

The simplest way of broadcasting to your clique is to take a male-to-male 3.5mm RCA audio cable, stick one end in the microphone jack of your computer and the other in the headphone jack, and get an account with Justin.tv or Ustream.tv. Your laptop will loop the audio output (from the headphone jack) to the audio input (from the mic jack) and broadcast it to whoever is on your stream. Now open your player of choice and play some old school jungle.

100.
A dark kitchen

A 'dark kitchen' may just sound like a health hazard, as unlikely as an al fresco dentist, but it in fact describes an entirely new type of structure. These informal kitchens, found on industrial estates and under major bridges nationwide, housed in shipping containers and railway arches, perhaps even port-a-loos, are thriving due to the sheer demand for fast food services. Established restaurants simply cannot cope with demand; this creates space for such guerrilla enterprises, who produce the fast food on their behalf.

In this context your shed is going to be a glamorous place in which to cook. If you don't want to freelance for your local fish and chippy or pizza place, then consider setting up your own dark shed kitchen, with second-hand industrial equipment and some serious extraction. You will be well placed to take a slice of the pie – takeaways are now worth a tasty £4.9 billion a year. Register with JustEat or UberEats and look to flyer in areas where people are overworked and overpaid.

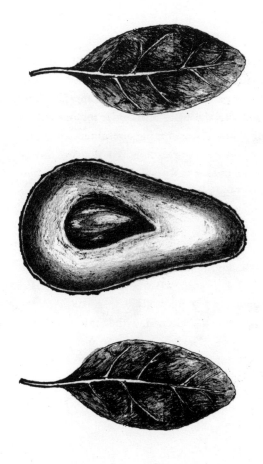

Shedonism

101.
The end of the shed

Each shed has a lifespan – you cannot take your shed with you when you go. By which I mean when you move. Or can you? In fact, there are various ways you might reposition or repurpose your outbuilding.

The most elegant recent example of this is Turner-Prize nominated artist Simon Starling's project Shedboatshed. Starling found an old wooden shed eight kilometres downstream of the Swiss town of Basel, dismantled it and turned it into a boat, before sailing it to a Basel museum where it was reconfigured into its original form.

If you are actually moving house, consider tweaking the above model to allow your own shed-boat to ferry loads of furniture up and down the canal to your new gaff, before sinking it in the waves.

You could also smash up your shed and keep the planks, using them as rustic decking in your new pad, or perhaps as simple garden furniture, each day walking happily over your past, like so many graves of past projects.

The simplest way to celebrate your outgoing shed, of course, is to burn it: it becomes its own ceremonial pyre. The hearty bonfire is a symbol of renewal. You may have had enough of smoking salmon. The occasion becomes a purge of failed enterprise, of dreams gone up in smoke, a sacrifice to the gods of the shed, and time to move on.